On Cats

Living on Luck: Selected Letters 1960s–1970s (Volume 2) (1995)

Betting on the Muse: Poems & Stories (1996)

Bone Palace Ballet: New Poems (1997)

The Captain Is Out to Lunch and the Sailors Have Taken Over the Ship (1998)

Reach for the Sun: Selected Letters 1978–1994 (Volume 3) (1999)

What Matters Most Is How Well You Walk Through the Fire: New Poems (1999)

Open All Night: New Poems (2000)

Night Torn Mad with Footsteps: New Poems (2001)

*Beerspit Night and Cursing: The Correspondence of Charles Bukowski &
 Sheri Martinelli 1960–1967 (2001)*

Sifting Through the Madness for the Word, the Line, the Way: New Poems (2003)

The Flash of Lightning Behind the Mountain: New Poems (2004)

Slouching Toward Nirvana (2005)

Come on In! (2006)

The People Look Like Flowers at Last (2007)

The Pleasures of the Damned (2007)

The Continual Condition (2009)

On Writing (2015)

On Cats (2015)

On Cats

CHARLES BUKOWSKI

Edited by Abel Debritto

ecco
An Imprint of HarperCollins*Publishers*

Photographs courtesy of Linda Lee Bukowski.

HarperCollins books may be purchased for educational, business, or sales promotional use. For information please e-mail the Special Markets Department at SPsales@harpercollins.com.

A hardcover edition of this book was published in 2015 by Ecco, an imprint of HarperCollins Publishers.

FIRST ECCO PAPERBACK EDITION PUBLISHED 2017.

Designed by Suet Yee Chong

Library of Congress Cataloging-in-Publication Data has been applied for.

ISBN 978-0-06-265143-3

23 24 25 26 27 LBC 14 13 12 11 10

Beeker

ſ

All the eating places were closed at that time of the night and it was a long ride into town. I couldn't take him back to my room, so I had to take a chance on Millie. She always had plenty of food. At any rate, she *always* had cheese.

I was right. She made us cheese sandwiches with coffee. The cat knew me and leaped into my lap.

I put the cat on the floor.

"Watch, Mr. Burnett," I said.

"Shake hands!" I said to the cat. "Shake hands!"

The cat just sat there.

"That's funny, it always used to do it," I said. "Shake hands!"

I remembered Shipkey had told Mr. Burnett that I talked to birds.

"Come on now! Shake hands!"

I began to feel foolish.

"Come on! Shake hands!"

I put my head right down by the cat's head and put everything I had into it.

"Shake hands!"

The cat just sat there.

I went back to my chair and picked up my cheese sandwich.

"Cats are funny animals, Mr. Burnett. You can never tell. Millie, put on Tchaikovsky's 6th for Mr. Burnett."

We listened to the music. Millie came over and sat in my lap. She just had on a negligee. She dropped down against me. I put my sandwich to one side.

"I want you to notice," I said to Mr. Burnett, "the section which brings forth the marching movement in this symphony. I think it's one of the most beautiful movements in all music. And besides its beauty and force, its structure is perfect. You can feel intelligence at work."

The cat jumped up into the lap of the man with the goatee. Millie laid her cheek against mine, put a hand on my chest. "Where ya been, baby boy? Millie's missed ya, ya know."

The record ended and the man with the goatee took the cat off his lap, got up and turned the record over. He should have found record #2 in the album. By turning it over we would get the climax rather early. I didn't say anything, though, and we listened to it end.

"How did you like it?" I asked.

"Fine! Just fine!"

He had the cat on the floor.

"Shake hands! Shake hands!" he said to the cat.

The cat shook hands.

"Look," he said, "I can make the cat shake hands."

"Shake hands!"

The cat rolled over.

"No, shake *hands*! Shake *hands*!"

The cat just sat there.

He put his head down by the cat's head and talked into its ear.

"Shake hands!"

The cat stuck its paw right into his goatee.

"Did you see? I made him shake hands!" Mr. Burnett seemed pleased.

Millie pressed tight against me. "Kiss me, baby boy," she said, "kiss me."

"No."

"Good Lord, ya gone off ya nut, baby boy? What's eatin' at ya? Sompin's botherin' ya tonight, I can tell! Tell Millie all about ut! Millie'd go ta hell for ya, baby boy, ya know that. Whats'a matter, huh? Ha?"

"Now I'll get the cat to roll over," said Mr. Burnett.

Millie wrapped her arms tight around me and peered down into my upward eye. She looked very sad and motherish and smelled like cheese. "Tell Millie what's eatin' ya up, baby boy."

"Roll over!" said Mr. Burnett to the cat.

The cat just sat there.

"Listen," I said to Millie, "see that man over there?"

"Yeah, I see him."

"Well, that's Whit Burnett."

"Who's that?"

"The magazine editor. The one I send my stories to."

"Ya mean the one who sends you those little tiny notes?"

"Rejection slips, Millie."

"Well, he's mean. I don't like him."

"Roll over!" said Mr. Burnett to the cat. The cat rolled over. "Look!" he yelled. "I made the cat roll over! I'd like to buy this cat! It's marvelous!"

Millie tightened her grip about me and peered down into my eye. I was quite helpless. I felt like a still live fish on ice in a butcher's counter on Friday morning.

"Listen," she said, "I can get him ta print one a ya stories. I can get him ta print *alla* them!"

"Watch me make the cat roll over!" said Mr. Burnett.

"No, no, Millie, you don't understand! Editors aren't like fixed businessmen. Editors have *scruples*!"

"Scruples?"

"Scruples."

"Roll over!" said Mr. Burnett.

The cat just sat there.

"I know all about ya *scruples*! Don't ya worry about scruples! Baby boy, I'll get him ta print *alla* ya stories!"

"Roll over!" said Mr. Burnett to the cat. Nothing happened.

"No, Millie, I won't have it."

She was all wound around me. It was hard to breathe and she was rather heavy. I felt my feet going to sleep. Millie pressed her check against mine and rubbed a hand up and down my chest. "Baby boy, ya got nothin' to say!"

Mr. Burnett put his head down by the cat's head and talked into its ear. "Roll over!"

The cat stuck its paw right into his goatee.

"I think this cat wants something to eat," he said.

With that, he got back into his chair. Millie went over and sat on his knee.

"Where'd ya get tha cute little goaty?" she asked.

"Pardon me," I said, "I'm going to get a drink of water."

I went in and sat in the breakfast nook and looked down at the flower designs on the table. I tried to scratch them off with a fingernail.

It was hard enough to share Millie's love with the cheese salesman and the welder. Millie with the figure right down to the hips. Damn, damn.

∫

A cat walks by and shakes Shakespeare
off his back.

I don't want to draw
like Mondrian,
I want to draw like a sparrow eaten by a cat.

∫

conversation on a telephone

I could tell by the crouch of the cat,
the way it was flattened,
that it was insane with prey;
and when my car came upon it,
it rose in the twilight
and made off
with bird in mouth,
a very large bird, gray,
the wings down like broken love,
the fangs in,
life still there
but not much,
not very much.

the broken love-bird
the cat walks in my mind
and I cannot make him out:
the phone rings,
I answer a voice,
but I see him again and again,
and the loose wings
the loose gray wings,
and this thing held
in a head that knows no mercy;
it is the world, it is ours;

I put the phone down
and the cat-sides of the room
come in upon me
and I would scream,
but they have places for people
who scream;
and the cat walks
the cat walks forever
in my brain.

I saw that bird and my hands were on the steering wheel and I saw
the wings and they were down like broken love, the wings said that,
and the cat moved away from the wheels of my car that way a cat
moves and I'm sick as I write this, and all the broken love of the
world and all the broken love birds, and the sky said this covered
with smog and cheap clouds and miscreant gods.

ʃ

I saw a bird when I was driving home from the track the other day.
It was in the mouth of a cat crouched down in the asphalt street,
the clouds overhead, the sunset, love and God overhead, and it saw
my car and rose, cat-rose insane, stiff back like mad love depravity,
and it walked toward the curbing, and I saw the bird, a large grey,
flop broken-winged, wings large and out, dipped, feathers spread,
still alive, cat-fanged; nobody saying anything, signals changing,
my motor running, and the wings the wings in my mind . . .

∫

the cat

this cat hangs around the iron fire escape
and she's yellow like the sun
and she's never seen a dog in that part
of the city, and boy, she's fat,
full of rats and tidbits from HARVEY'S BAR
and I've been going up the fire escape
to see this lady in the hotel
and she shows me letters from her son
in France, and it is a very small room
full of wine bottles and sadness,
and sometimes I leave her a little money,
and when I go down the fire escape
there's the cat again and
she rubs against my legs and
as I go to the car
she follows, and I've got to be careful
when I start up, but not too much so:
she's pretty smart, she knows
the car is not her friend.
and one day I went to see the lady
and she was dead. I mean, she wasn't there,
her room was empty. it had been a hemorrhage
I was told. and the room was now for rent.
well, there's no use being sad. I went down
the iron steps and there was the cat. I

picked her up and rubbed her, but oddly,
it was not the same cat. her fur was rough
and the eyes were mean. I threw it to the ground
and watched it run off and glare at me.
then I got into the car
and drove away.

Feathers

∫

The Arabians admire the cat, look down upon women and dogs because they show affection and affection is, some think, a sign of weakness. Well, perhaps it is. I do not show too much. My wives and girlfriends complain because I hold my soul separately—and give my body, perhaps, puritanically; but back to the g.d. cat. A cat is only ITSELF. That is why when it gets the poor bird it won't let go. This is a representative of the strong forces of LIFE that won't let go. The cat is the beutiful devil. And here we can use the word, even without the "a." You can get some dogs and some women to let go—and they'll let go. But a cat, hell, the lightning sides of houses will long be done over and he will still be purring in his milk. A cat will eat you when you die. No matter how long you've lived together. There was an old man once who died alone like Buk, and he dina have a woman but he hadda cat and he died it alone and it was days days days poor ol man began to stink, it not his fault, but the earth revolving and removing remains of what shoulda been buried by living earth spirits, and cat smelled good, to him, stink of dead meat, and when they found them the cat was clawing up from the floor, stuck to the bottom of the mattress like a rock, eating through the

mattress, hung like a clam on the rock, and they couldn't club him off or pry him off or burn him off, and they just hadda throw him off and away with the damned mattress. I suppose one moonlit nite through the dew of moon and leaves cooling the smell of death, he let go.

There are no spirits or gods in a cat, don't look for them, Shed. A cat is the picture of the eternal machinery, like the sea. You don't pet the sea because it's pretty but you pet a cat—why?— ONLY BECAUSE HE'LL LET YOU. And a cat never knows fear— finally—he only winds up into the spring of the sea and the rock, and even in a death-fight he does not think of anything except the majesty of darkness.

∫

I do not always hate the cat that kills the bird,
 only the cat
 that kills me . . .

friend moon, friend cat, you ask no mercy or gigs or gifts,
only lull and lavender. and houses. brush. movement
as in a bowl.
 oh young men of Princeton puffing pipes
 oh young men of Harvard puffing
 .scratching books for security,
for friend moon, friend cat
 you have no justification
 you are just pink puffs and pastels
 clouds
useless as my girlfriend's underwear upon the floor
or my girlfriend upon the floor
puffing for explosion
 like Ottorino Respighi's *Pines of Rome*.

. . . tree fulla birds makes justice.
or ground fulla worms.
or people fulla ground.

justification.

we walk upon a midnight's rug
neither drunk nor dreamed nor drugged.
and when the window bangs down
with the hauter and fart of the cannon
or the honk puffs the horn like a phallus
or the rhinoceros roars in his ice cream dream,

roars like the hair on your arm
putting down the needle on Kabalevsky's *The Comedians*
as dimes begin to breathe
and Poor ol' Dolores Costello
is rolled up on an old reel in the closet
like fishstring.

I'm with you . . . friend moon and cat:
we turn an ear, an eye,
calm in their story, then
move on, moon and cat

past
the old maid's burning
past Van Goghs and Rembrandts
hanging like leaves . . .

to the top of the roof, tonight;
to continents of exactness,
to the sound that spins the world.

∫

Small birds who go the way of cats sing on inside my head.

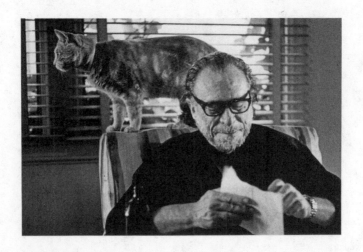

∫

startled into life like fire

in grievous deity my cat
walks around

he walks around and around
with electric tail and
push-button
eyes

he is
alive and
plush and
final as a plum
tree

neither of us understands
cathedrals or
the man outside
watering his
lawn

if I were all the man
that he is cat—
if there were men like this
the world could
begin

he leaps up on the couch
and walks through
porticoes of my
admiration.

∫

I was born to hustle roses down the avenues of the dead

2

you missed a cat argument the grey was
tired mad flipping tail and he monkied
with the black one who didn't want to
be bothered and then the black one
chased the grey one pawed it once the
grey one said *yow*
ran away stopped scratched its ear
flicked at a straw popped in air and
ran off defeated and planning as a
white one (another one) ran along the
other side of the fence chasing a
grasshopper as somebody shot Mr
Kennedy.

∫

The factories, the jails, the drunken days and nights, the hospitals have weakened and shaken me like a mouse in the mouth of a hip-cat: life.

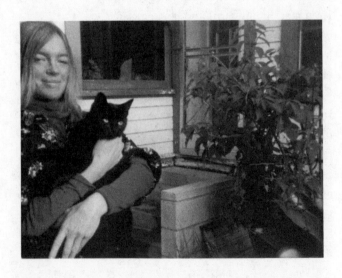

∫

the devious good of rescuing the suffering

once very thin and nervous
like a starving musician
I fed him well
and he has gotten fat
like a Texas oilman and not so
nervous
but still
odd.

asleep in bed I will awaken
and his nose will be touching my
nose and those
yellow great eyes
P O U R I N G
down into what's left of my soul
and then I will say—
 off, bastard!
 get your nose away from my
 nose!
purring like a spider full of
flies he will walk off a
little.

I was in the bathtub yesterday
and he came walking in

high on his feet
tail flicking
and I am in there
smoking a cigar and reading the
NEW YORKER
and he leaped up on the edge of the
tub
balancing on the slippery ivory
curving
and I told him,
 sir, you are a cat and cats
 don't like water.
but he went around to the faucets
and he hung there with his black feet
and the other part of him was
head down
sniffing at the water and the water was
HOT and he started drinking it
the thin red tongue
bashful and miraculous
dipping into the hot water
and he kept
sniffing
wondering what I was doing in there
what I found so good about it
and then that fat white fool
fell in! —
we all came out of there
wet and fast;
cat, me, cigar and NEW YORKER
spitting, screaming, sputtering, soaked
and my wife ran in

MY GOD! WHAT HAPPENED? WHAT HAPPENED?
I spoke through my unraveling cigar:
 a man can't even have a little privacy
 in his own bathtub, that's what!
she only laughed at us
and the cat was not even angry
he was still wet and fat
except for his tail
which now looked almost as thin as a
rat's tail and very sad and
he began licking
himself.
I used a towel,
then I walked into the bedroom
got into bed
and tried to find my place in the
magazine.

but the good mood was broken
I put the publication down
and stared up at the ceiling
up into space where God was supposed to
be
then I heard it:
MEEYOWW!

the next stray cat who comes to my door will
remain a
stray.

∫

portrait of a soul for flies

he is a man in a thinning undershirt of faded
revolution
advancing the mathematics of his impurity to the
final zero
and awakening this morning with the taste of salmon
on my tongue
I thought of him
although I felt like I needed a priest
or at least his housewoman
to stroke my private parts back to some speck of
majesty

there is a letter in his hand
from a rich man in Santa Fe:
"you're slipping, you're slipping, V. and I
who have been fans of yours for years
are seriously worried about your artistic
decline—even tho your popularity still seems to be
climbing. why don't you see a psychiatrist and get the
cork blown out of your
ass?
 J."

the Alka-Seltzer tablets spider-crawl to life
as his white cat sits inside the window
looking at him

my cat looks good, he thinks,
my cat doesn't have to keep MAKING IT
in the all-American grind
and he puts his nose
his all-American nose
into the sharp bubbles the cat never needs
and drinks the bubbles
while sweat of last night's 18 beers and pint of scotch
moil down his ears and neck

I should call Fat Freddy the Turdhurler
I should find a brass mountain to hide my costermonger's
psyche under

a bird rises in the brush outside
caught between the sun and himself
and the shade of a huge wing-shadow
passes over him
passes over the house-edge—

the cat leaps against the screen
and everything is older than Normandy and Stalingrad
and the shelling of the harbors

Winston Churchill
with child's brain
spittle on his chin
waves to the love-fogged crowd
from the tall window
and then he's dead
like almost everything
else

but the man in the thinning undershirt:
his cat is angry
the screen has cheated him
and the cat's yellow eyes come down to his
like the eyes of a small businessman
who once fired him for loafing in the
stockroom

"shit on you," he tells the cat, "and
shit on all the untalented demeanors of my
dwindling talent."

30 minutes later
that first bottle of beer
is better than any sex anywhere in the world
with any big-assed cow
that he ever ripped the silk and lace
from

he goes into the bedroom where his woman sits
rocking his child in her belly
and he takes the cigarette out of her hand
puts it to his mouth
and coughs coughs coughs
and still the dwindling talent
he thinks, I've heard that cough before:
a horse chunking wash of saliva past iron bit
while pulling his first junkwagon
through a frosty useless morning
in some small city
where only one man owns a
Mercedes

he is sweating
he must stink
but the walls are polite
and he holds one half a beer in a bottle
and the woman says,
"I hope you didn't mean all those things you said
last night."

"ah, just the good things."

"well, that narrows it down.
you're not going to drink today?"

"just a little, sweetie. I'm a coward."

"feed the cat."

"yeah."

at the door is a Western Union boy. he gives him an
unsubstantial tip and the boy runs off
sweating
the American hustler
God save him

THE DEADLINE FOR OUR ORIGINAL POETRY ISSUE
OUT IN SEPTEMBER IS AUGUST 17TH WOULD
APPRECIATE YOUR CONTRIBUTING TO THIS
UNIQUE ISSUE BEST WISHES
 GENE COLE INTERMISSION MAGAZINE
 3212 NORTH BROADWAY
 CHICAGO
ILL

"did somebody die?"

he hands her the
telegram

"ooo, you're famous!"

"I can see it now: me and Genet and Sartre
sharing a drink at a sidewalk cafe in
Paree."

"who are they?"

"nobody. other genii."

"oh. well, feed the
cat."

so I fed the cat
drank 18 more cans of beer and
wrote
this.

∫

sensible brush, sleeping
flower, I awaken

the hunter goes by my window
4 feet locked in the bright stillness of a
yellow and blue
night.

cruel strangeness takes hold in wars, in
gardens—
the yellow and blue night explodes before
me, atomic, surgical,
full of starlit salty
devils . . .

then the cat leaps up on the
fence, a tubby dismay,
stupid, lonely . . .
whiskers like an old lady in the
supermarket
and naked as the
moon.

I am temporarily
delighted.

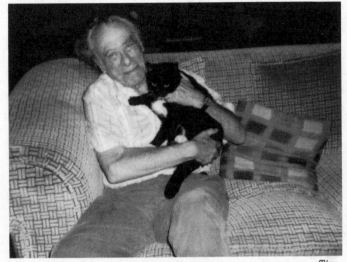

Ting

ʃ

I don't like love as a command, as a search. it must come to you, like a hungry cat at the door.

∫

the mockingbird

the mockingbird had been following the cat
all summer
mocking mocking mocking
teasing and cocksure;
the cat crawled under rockers on porches
tail flashing
and said something very angry to the mockingbird
which I didn't understand.

yesterday the cat walked calmly up the driveway
with the mockingbird alive in its mouth,
wings fanned, beautiful wings fanned and flopping,
feathers parted like a woman's legs in sex,
and the bird was no longer mocking,
it was asking, it was praying
but the cat
striding down through centuries
would not listen.

I saw it crawl under a yellow car
with the bird
to bargain it to another place.

summer was over.

∫

looking at the cat's balls

sitting here by the window
sweating beer sweat
mauled by the summer
I am looking at the cat's balls.

it's not my choice.
he sleeps in an old rocker
on the porch
and there he looks at me—
from behind—
hung to his cat's balls.

there's his tail, damned thing,
hanging out of the
way—
I view his furry storage tanks—
what can a man think about
while looking at a cat's nuts?
certainly not the sunken navies of
great sea battles.
certainly not a program to aid the
poor.
certainly not a flower market or a dozen
eggs.
certainly not a broken light switch.

balls iz balls, that's all—
and most *certainly* a cat's balls,
my own are rather mushy-looking,
and, I'm told by my contemporaries,
quite large:
"you've got a lot of balls, Bukowski!"

but the cat's balls:
I can't figure whether he's hung to them
or whether they're hung to him—
you see, there is this almost nightly battle for
the female—
and it doesn't come easy for any of us.

you see there—
a piece is missing from his left ear;
one time I thought one of his eyes had been
clawed out
but when the mass of dried blood peeled away
a week later
there was this pure
gold green eye
looking at me.

his entire body is sore from bites
and the other day,
attempting to pet his head
he yowled and almost bit me—
that fur skin around his skull, bloodless,
had been split to reveal the bone.
it doesn't come easy for any of us.
those cat's balls, poor fellow.

he sleeps now dreaming—
what?—a fat mockingbird in his mouth?—
or surrounded by cat bitches in heat?—
he dreams his daydreams
and will find out
tonight.

good luck, old fellow,
it doesn't come easy,
hung to our balls we are, that's it,
we're hung to our balls,
and I could use a little myself—
meanwhile—
watch the eyes and lead with the left
and run like hell
when it just isn't any use
anymore.

∫

the strangest thing

I was sitting in a chair in the dark
the other night
not doing anything
when the most horrible sounds of torture
began in the brush
outside my
window.
it was obviously not a male cat and a female
cat but
a male and a
male
and from the sound
one appeared to be
much larger and attacking
with all intent to
kill.
I sat. then it
stopped.

then it began again
worse this time;
the sounds were so terrible
that I was unable to
move.

then it stopped again.

I got up from my chair
went to bed and
slept.

I had a dream. this small, very small
cat came to me in my dream
and it was very
sad. it spoke to me, it said:
"look what that other cat did to me."
and it turned on my lap
and I saw the slashes and
indentations. then it jumped
off my lap.

then that was all.

I awakened at 8:45 p.m.
put on my clothes and walked outside and
looked around.

there was nothing there.
I walked back inside and dropped two eggs
into a pot of water
and turned up the
burner.

∫

wet night

the rag.
she sat there, glooming.
I couldn't do anything with her.
it was raining.
she got up and left.
well, hell, here it is again, I thought.
I picked up my drink and turned the radio up,
took the lampshade off the lamp
and smoked a cheap black bitter cigar
imported from Germany.
there was a knock on the door
and I opened the door
a little man stood in the rain
and he said,
have you seen a pigeon on your porch?
I told him I hadn't seen a pigeon on my porch
and he said if I saw a pigeon on my porch
to let him know.
I closed the door
sat down
and then a black cat leaped through the
window and jumped on my
lap and purred, it was a beautiful animal
and I took it into the kitchen and we both ate a
slice of ham.

then I turned off all the lights
and went to bed
and that black cat went to bed with me
and it purred
and I thought, well, somebody likes me,
then the cat started pissing,
it pissed all over me and all over the sheets,
the piss rolled across my belly and slid down my sides
and I said: hey, what's wrong with you?
I picked up the cat and walked him to the door
and threw him out into the rain
and I thought, that's very strange, that cat
pissing on me
his piss was cold as the rain.
then I phoned her
and I said, look, what's wrong with you? have you lost
your god damned mind?
I hung up and pulled the sheets off the bed
and got in and lay there listening to the rain.
sometimes a man doesn't know what to do about things
and sometimes it's best to lie very still
and try not to think at all
about anything.

that cat belonged to somebody
it had a flea collar.
I don't know about the
woman.

∫

[. . .]
cats kill cats at
3 a.m. in the morning
chewing off the front
legs and getting to the
throat
leaving fur
and stiffened bone
for any collector of
garbage and life
past gone.

∫

little tigers everywhere

Sam the whorehouse man
has squeaky shoes
and he walks up and down
the court
squeaking and talking to
the cats.
he's 310 pounds,
a killer
and he talks to the cats.
he sees the women at the massage
parlor and has no girlfriends
no automobile
he doesn't drink or dope
his biggest vices are
chewing on a cigar and
feeding all the cats in
the neighborhood.
some of the cats get
pregnant
and so finally there are
more and more cats and
every time I open my door
one or two cats will
run in and sometimes I'll
forget they are there and

they'll shit under the bed
or I'll awaken at night
hearing sounds
leap up with my blade
sneak into the kitchen and
find one of Sam the whorehouse
man's cats walking around on
the sink or sitting on top
of the refrigerator.

Sam runs the love parlor
around the corner
and his girls stand in the
doorway in the sun
and the traffic signals go
red and green and red and green
and all of Sam's cats
possess some of the meaning
as do the days and the nights.

∫

love is the crushed cats
of the universe

*Sent to Sheri Martinelli in 1966, this is the only known drawing of a cat by
Bukowski. Other attempts at illustrating cats, such as the painting on the title
page, came out as dogs.*

∫

I walked into the kitchen, opened a bottle of vitamin E, 400 I.U. each, and downed several with half a glass of Perrier water. It was going to be a good night for Chinaski. The sun was slanting down through the Venetian blinds, making a familiar pattern on the carpet, and the white wine was chilling in the refrigerator.

I opened the door and walked out on the porch. There was a strange cat out there. He was a huge creature, a tom, with a shining black coat and luminous yellow eyes. He wasn't frightened of me. He walked up purring and rubbed against one of my legs. I was a good guy and he knew it. Animals knew things like that. They had an instinct. I walked back inside and he followed me.

I opened him up a can of StarKist solid white tuna. Packed in spring water. Net wt. 7 oz.

∫

bad fix

old Butch, they fixed him,
the girls don't look like much
anymore.

when Big Sam moved out
of the back
I inherited big Butch,
70 as cats go,
old,
fixed,
but still as big and
mean a cat as anybody
ever remembered
seeing.

he's damn near gnawed
off my hand
the hand that feeds him
a couple of
times
but I've forgiven him,
he's fixed
and there's something about
him
that doesn't like
it.

at night
I hear him mauling and
running other cats through
the brush.
Butch, he's still a magnificent
old cat,
fighting
even without it.

what a bastard he must have been
with it
when he was 19 or 20
walking slowly down
his path
and I even look at him
now
still feel the courage
and the strength
in spite of man's smallness
in spite of man's scientific
divinity,
old Butch
retains
endures

peering at me with those
evil yellow eyes
out of that huge
undefeated
head.

∫

gift

you know
the man in back moved out
couldn't get his rent
so I inherited this
huge old cat
big as an average dog
mean
yellow eyes
old and furiously strong
when he strikes with one of those
paws
the walls shake.
his name is "Butch" and he
doesn't play around
he's cranky
has his own set ideas
learned from somewhere
long ago.
he gets on the trip
which is his
sometimes he gets
gone
I'll be petting him
and then he'll have me
my hand trapped in his

gut
the teeth will incise into
the top part of my hand
and holding me there
like that
he'll rip the backs of
my wrists
with his two rear paws
with the claws
fully extended . . .
I leave my hand there
until he's finished
then I
lift it away
rivulets of blood
seep . . . he just
looks at me.

I'll send him to you
in a whole natural almond
crate
I'll cut holes so he can
breathe

but beware when you pry off
the lid

I'll send him to you
just in time
via Air Express

open that crate on
National Poetry Day.

∫

Butch Van Gogh

just before leaving Hollywood my cat got into a fight
leaving him with a cauliflower ear.
now in this new place
I took him to a vet yesterday.
they had animal dentistry
shrinks for animals
plus an EMERGENCY room
he had to have surgery
anesthesia
pills
ointments.

the bill
came to $82.50.

"Jesus," I told the vet, "this is a ten-year-old
de-balled alley cat. I can get a dozen of these for
nothing."

the vet just made little circles on a piece of paper
with his pencil.

"all right," I said, "go ahead."

"Butch Bukowski," the vet wrote down the patient's name.

when I went back to get him they had his skull wrapped
and
he looked like he had a hole drilled in his head.
he was carried out of room 6 by a nurse.

"what'd you do?" I asked, "give him a lobotomy?"

now he just sits on top of the stove and stares at me.
Butch Van Gogh Artaud Bukowski.

like a friend of mine once told me:
"man, everything you touch turns to shit!"

he's right.
I've been masturbating since I was eleven years
old.

∫

a reader

my cat shit in my archives
he climbed into my *Golden State Sunkist*
orange box
and he shit on my poems
my original poems
saved for the university archives.

that one-eared fat black critic
he signed me off.

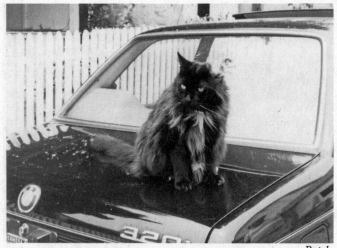

Butch

∫

Manx

this is just a long call
from a short space.
it doesn't engender up
any special brilliance
to know that
we are going wrong again.
we laugh less and less,
become more sane.
all we want is
the absence of others.
even the classical music
has been heard too often,
the good books have been
read.
we suspect again
as we did in the beginning
that we are
odd, deformed, fit
nowhere here . . .
as we write this
there is an ugly buzzing
something lands in our
hair
becomes embedded there.
we reach up

yank it free
as it bites our finger.
what damned nonentity
is this
in the middle of
the night?
it's gone . . .

there is a sliding
glass door
and we see outside
a white Manx sitting there
with one crossed eye.
his tongue sticks out
sidewise.
we pull the door open
and he slides in
front legs running
in one direction,
rear
in the other.
he makes it towards us
in a scurvy angle
runs up our legs
our chest
places front legs
like arms
near our shoulders
sticks his snout
quite near our nose
and looks at us
best he can;

also befuddled,
we look back.

some night,
old boy,
some time,
some way.
stuck together
here.

we smile again
like we used to.
suddenly the Manx
leaps away
scattering across the
rug sideways
chasing something
that none of us
can see.

An international thief ran over my favorite cat Monday
(the Manx). The whole front wheel of the car ran over
him. He's laying up in the hospital now. The doc says it's
possible he may never walk again. Too early to know.
The x-rays show the backbone fucked up. A great cat.
Real personality. Maybe they can operate, or build him
a set of wheels. The x-rays also show somebody shot the
cat some time in the past. He's had a tough go.

ʃ

The Manx is walking again, although a bit sideways. He was in the cat hospital for 7 days. The Doc says it's a miracle, he never expected the Manx to walk again. Also, he ain't a Manx, somebody cut his tail off. He's part Siamese. One very strange animal, intelligent as hell. The guy who ran him over came by last night, Manx took one look and ran, shot up the stairway and hid behind the toilet upstairs. He knew who was driving that car.

∫

Now here's a beautiful cat. Its tongue hangs out, it's cross-eyed. Its tail is chopped off. He's beautiful, he's got sense. We took him to the vet to have him x-rayed—he got hit by a car. The doctor says, 'This cat's been run over twice, he's been shot, his tail's been cut off.' I said, 'This cat is me.' He came to the door starving to death. He knew right where to come. We're both bums off the street.

∫

The Manx came to the door almost dead one day. We took him in, fattened him up, then a friend came by drunk and ran him over with his car. I saw it. The cat just stared at me as it was happening. We took him to the vet. X-rays. He's not a Manx at all. Vet says somebody cut off his tail. Also he's been shot, pellet still lodged and he was run over, once before—mend of backbone in x-rays. He's also cross-eyed. Said he'd probably never walk again. Now he's running, tongue hanging out, cross-eyed. He's a tough crazy.

Manx

∫

The tailless, cross-eyed cat came to the door one day, and
we let him in. Old pink eyes. Quite a guy. Animals are
inspirational. They don't know how to lie. They are natural
forces. TV can make me ill in five minutes, but I can look at
an animal for hours and find nothing but grace and glory,
life as it should be.

∫

night work

my cat leaped into the fireplace
burning
as Van Gogh
slit the rear screen
and entered
looking for the blue whore
of nowhere.

∫

One day I was standing around, waiting as usual, not friendly with the gang, no longer really wanting to be, when Gene rushed up to me, "Hey, Henry, come on!"

"What is it?"

"COME ON!"

Gene started running and I ran after him. We ran down the driveway and into the Gibsons' backyard. The Gibsons had a large brick wall all around their backyard.

"LOOK! HE'S GOT THE CAT CORNERED! HE'S GOING TO KILL IT!"

There was a small white cat backed into a corner of the wall. It couldn't go up and it couldn't go in one direction or the other. Its back was arched and it was spitting, its claws ready. But it was very small and Chuck's bulldog, Barney, was growling and moving closer and closer. I got the feeling that the cat had been put there by the guys and then the bulldog had been brought in. I felt it strongly because of the way Chuck and Eddie and Gene were watching: they had a guilty look.

"You guys did this," I said.

"No," said Chuck, "it's the cat's fault. It came in here. Let it fight its way out."

"I hate you bastards," I said.

"Barney's going to kill that cat," said Gene.

"Barney will rip it to pieces," said Eddie. "He's afraid of the claws but when he moves in it will be all over."

Barney was a large brown bulldog with slobbering jaws. He was dumb and fat with senseless brown eyes. His growl was steady and he kept inching forward, the hairs standing up on his neck and along his back. I felt like kicking him in his stupid ass but I figured he would rip my leg off. He was entirely intent upon the kill. The white cat wasn't even fully grown. It hissed and waited, pressed against the wall, a beautiful creature, so clean. The dog moved slowly forward. Why did the guys need this? This wasn't a matter of courage, it was just dirty play. Where were the grown-ups? Where were the authorities? They were always around accusing me. Now where were they? I thought of rushing in, grabbing the cat and running, but I didn't have the nerve. I was afraid that the bulldog would attack me. The knowledge that I didn't have the courage to do what was necessary made me feel terrible. I began to feel physically sick. I was weak. I didn't want it to happen yet I couldn't think of any way to stop it.

"Chuck," I said, "let the cat go, please. Call your dog off."

Chuck didn't answer. He just kept watching.

Then he said, "Barney, go get him! Get that cat!"

Barney moved forward and suddenly the cat leaped. It was a furious blur of white and hissing, claws and teeth. Barney backed off and the cat retreated to the wall again.

"Go get him, Barney," Chuck said again.

"God damn you, shut up!" I told him.

"Don't talk to me that way," Chuck said.

Barney began to move in again.

"You guys set this up," I said.

I heard a slight sound behind us and looked around. I saw old Mr. Gibson watching from behind his bedroom window. He wanted the cat to get killed too, just like the guys. Why? Old Mr. Gibson was our mailman with the false teeth. He had a wife who stayed in the house all the time. She only came out to empty the garbage. Mrs. Gibson always wore a net over her hair and she was always dressed in a nightgown, bathrobe and slippers.

Then as I watched, Mrs. Gibson, dressed as always, came and stood next to her husband, waiting for the kill. Old Mr. Gibson was one of the few men in the neighborhood with a job but he still needed to see the cat killed. Gibson was just like Chuck, Eddie and Gene. There were too many of them.

The bulldog moved closer. I couldn't watch the kill. I felt a great shame at leaving the cat like that. There was always the chance that the cat might try to escape, but I knew that they would prevent it. That cat wasn't only facing the bulldog, it was facing Humanity.

I turned and walked away, out of the yard, up the driveway and to the sidewalk. I walked along the sidewalk toward where I lived and there in the front yard of his home, my father stood waiting.

"Where have you been?" he asked.

I didn't answer.

"Get inside," he said, "and stop looking so unhappy or I'll give you something that will really make you unhappy!"

∫

cats and people and you and me and
everything—

the Egyptians loved the cat
were often entombed with it
instead of the woman
and never the dog

and now
here
the good people with the
good eyes
are very few

yet the fine cats
with great style
lounge about
in the alleys of
the universe.

about
our argument tonight
whatever it was
about
and
no matter
how unhappy

it made us
feel

remember that
there is a
cat
somewhere
adjusting to the
space of itself
with a delightful
wonderment of
easiness.

in other words
magic persists
without us
no matter what
we do
against it.

and I would plunder and
destroy the last chance of
myself and of you

that this might
continue.

there is no
argument.

∫

I find my place, pull into the driveway, park it, get out, just another old matador. But inside, as I open the door, my favorite white cat, *The Jinx*, leaps up into my arms and suddenly I am in love again.

Ting

∫

the history of a tough motherfucker

he came to the door one night wet boney beaten and
terrorized.
a white cross-eyed tailless cat
I took him in and fed him and he stayed
got to trust until a friend drove up the driveway
and ran him over
I took what was left to a vet who said, "not much
chance . . . give him these pills and wait . . . his backbone
is crushed, it was crushed once before but somehow
melded, if he lives he'll never walk again, look at
these x-rays, he's been shot, look here, the pellets
are still in him . . . also, he once had a tail, somebody
cut it off . . ."

I took the cat back, it was a hot summer, one of the
hottest summers in decades, I put him on the bathroom
floor, gave him water and pills, he wouldn't eat, he
wouldn't touch the water, I dipped my finger into it
and wet his mouth and I talked to him, I didn't go any-
where, I put in a lot of bathroom time and I talked to
him and gently touched him and he just looked back at
me with those pale blue crossed eyes as the days went
by he made his first move
dragging himself forward by his front legs
(the rear ones wouldn't move)

he made it to the litter box
crawled over and in,
that was like the horns of chance and possible victory
blowing away in the bathroom and into the city, I
related to that cat—I'd had it bad, not that kind of
bad but bad enough . . .

one morning he got up, stood up, fell back down and he
just looked at me.

"you make it, man," I said to him, "you're a good one . . ."

he kept trying it, getting up and falling down, finally
he walked a few steps, he was like a drunk weaving, the
rear legs just didn't want to do it and he fell again, rested,
then got up . . .

you know the rest: now he's better than ever, cross-eyed,
almost toothless, all the grace is back, and that look in
the eyes never left . . .

and now sometimes I'm interviewed, they want to hear about
life and literature and I get drunk and hold up my cross-eyed
shot runover de-tailed cat before them and I say, "look, look
at *this*!"

but they don't understand, they say something like, "you
say you've been influenced by Celine . . ."

"no," I hold the cat up before them, "by what happens, by
things like this, by this, by *this*! . . ."

I wobble the cat, holding him up under the front legs in
the smokey and drunken light; he's relaxed, he knows things . . .

it's about then that almost all the interviews end.
although I am very proud sometimes when I see the interviews
later and there I am and there is the cat and we are photo-
graphed together . . .

he knows it's bullshit too but it helps get the old catfood,
right?

∫

terminology

my other favorite cat
seemed to be dying
and I had him in and
out of the
vet's place
for x-rays,
consultations,
injections,
operations,
"anything at all,"
I told the doc,
"let's try to keep
him going . . ."

one morning
I drove over
to pick him up
and the girl at the
counter
a vast girl
in a wrap-around white
nurse's outfit
asked me,
"do you want your
cat put to sleep?"

"what?" I
asked.

she repeated
her statement.

"put to sleep?" I
asked, "you mean
exterminated?"

"well, yes," she
smiled under her
tiny eyes, then
looking at the
card in her
hand she said,
"oh no, I see it
was *Mrs. Evans*
who wanted it
done to her
cat . . ."

"really?" I
asked.

"I'm sorry,"
she said.

she walked into
the other room with
her card
and I thought,

you're sorry and I'm
sorry,
and your sorry
fat ass
your sorry
walk
your sorry
bed
your sorry
life and your
sorry death
and your sorry
Mrs. Evans
and both of your
sorry fat
shits.

then I walked
over,
sat down
and opened up
a cat
magazine, then
closed it,
thinking, it's just
her job; it's
done.
she doesn't kill
the cats,
she records the
messages.

when she came out
into the office
she no longer quite
disgusted me
and I opened the
cat magazine
again
and turned the
pages
as if I had
forgotten
everything,
which I
hadn't,
exactly.

∫

one for the old boy

he was just a
cat
cross-eyed,
a dirty white
with pale blue eyes

I won't bore you with his
history
just to say
he had much bad luck
and was a good old
guy
and he died
like people die
like elephants die
like rats die
like flowers die
like water evaporates and
the wind stops blowing

the lungs gave out
last Monday.
now he's in the rose
garden
and I've heard a

stirring march
playing for him
inside of me
which I know
not many
but some of you
would like to
know
about.

that's
all.

Manx

∫

a nature poem for you

I've got these two kittens who are rapidly growing into
cats and
we sleep on the same bed—the problem being that
they are early risers:
I am often awakened by claws running across my
face.

these,
all they do is run, eat, sleep, shit and
fight
but at moments they are still and they look
at me
with eyes
far more beautiful than any human eyes I have ever
seen.
they are good guys.

late at night when I drink and type
they are about
like say
one on the back of my chair and the other down there
nibbling at my toes.
we have a natural concern for each other, like to know
where we are and where everything
is.

then
they come out
run across the floor
run across the typed sheets there
leaving wrinkles and tiny puncture-holes in the
paper.

then
they leap into the big box of letters I get from
people
but they don't answer, they are house-
broken.

I expect any number of cat poems from them
of which this is the
first.

"my god," they will say, "all Chinaski writes about
are cats!"
"my god," they used to say, "all Chinaski writes about
are whores!"

the complainers will complain and keep buying my
books: they love the way I irritate
them.

this is the last poem of any number of poems
tonight, there's
one drink of wine left
and both of those guys
they are asleep across the top of my feet.
I can feel the gentle weight of them

the touch of fur
I am aware of their breathing:
good things happen often, remember that
as the Bombs trundle out in their magnificent
dumbness
these
at my feet
know more,
are
more,
and instants of the moment explode
larger
and a lucky past
can never be
killed.

∫

a sensible fellow

when I fart
my cat could care
less.

Bhau

∫

wearing the collar

I live with a lady and four cats
and some days we all get
along.

some days I have trouble with
one of the
cats.

other days I have trouble with
two of the
cats.

other days,
three.

some days I have trouble with
all four of the
cats

and the
lady:

ten eyes looking at me
as if I were a dog.

∫

exactly fine

the strays keep arriving: now we have 5
cats and they are tenuous, flighty, con-
ceited, naturally bright and awesomely
beautiful.

one of the finest things about cats is
that when you're feeling bad, very bad—
if you just look at a cat cooling it
the way they do
it's a lesson in persevering against
the odds, and
if you can look at 5 cats that's 5
times better.

no matter the dozens of cans of tuna
from the supermarket: it's fuel for
an untapped dignity—a splendid
sleek energy of
YEA
especially when it all becomes too
much: this over-thought upon the
happenings of
humans.

∫

In the morning we awakened, man and wife, as so many
people do. But there was a new cat, a 5th cat, a very young
fellow who had entered our family that night. He was ter-
rorized by life, hungry, lonely. Somehow in our drunken-
ness, we had fed him. Now, down on the rug, he whirled
about, leaped in joy and in some panic of the newness of
things, he looked at us with his wild yellow eyes.

A good sign: a new life, like ours.

Then I thought, today Linda Lee will eat something
besides that cheesecake wedding cake (the remainder of
which was jammed into the refrigerator).

And someday we will see all those many wedding
photos and we will live it all over again and ingest, once
again, the crazy magic.

"Good morning, Mrs. Bukowski," I said, rather laugh-
ing.

"Good morning, dear husband," Linda Lee answered,
rather laughing back.

And we had this new door in the side of our house.
And many more doors to open.

\int

a cat is a cat is a cat is a cat

she's whistling and clapping
for the cats
at 2 a.m.
as I sit in here
with my wine and my
Beethoven.

"they're just prowling," I
tell her . . .

Beethoven rattles his bones
in majesty.

and those damn cats
don't even care
about
any of that.

and
if they did
I wouldn't like them
at
all:

things begin to lose their
natural value
as they near
human
endeavor.

nothing against
Beethoven:

he did fine
for what he
was

but I wouldn't want
him
on my rug
with one leg
over his head
while
he was
licking
his balls.

ʃ

another casualty

cat got run over
now silver screw holding together a broken
femur
right leg
bound in bright red
bandage

got cat home from vet's
took my eye off
him for
a moment

he ran across floor
dragging his red
leg
chasing the female
cat

worst thing the
fucker could
do

he's in the penalty
box
now

sweating it
out

he's just like the
rest of
us

he has these large
yellow eyes
staring

only wanting to
live the
good
life.

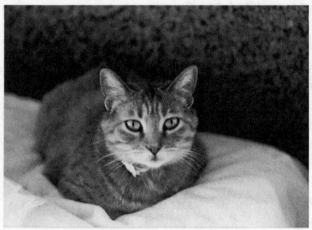

Beauty

∫

my cat, the writer

as I sit in front of this
machine
my cat Ting sits behind
me
on the back of my
chair.

now
as I type this
he
steps upon an open
drawer
and then out across this
desk.

now
his nose is over this
paper
and he watches me
type.

then
he leaves off
goes
over and sticks his nose into

a
coffee cup.

now
he's back
his head across this piece of
paper.
he
sticks his paw down into the
ribbon.

I
hit a key and
he
leaps away.

now
he just sits and watches me
type.
I've moved my wineglass and
bottle
to the other side of
the
machine.

the radio plays bad
piano
music.

Ting just sits and looks at
this
typer.

do you think he wants to be
a
writer?
or was he one in the
past?

I
dislike cute cat
poems
but I've written one
anyhow.

now
there's a fly in
here
and Ting watches his every
move.

it's 11:45 p.m. and
I'm
drunk . . .

listen, relax, you've read
worse
poems than
this . . .

and I've written
them.

∫

5 cats

cat A: old granny, pointed teeth, she's seen too
much, she doesn't give a damn about the Russian
Revolution or any others; Harry Truman playing the
piano with Lauren Bacall plopped thereupon doesn't
matter; she's mean because to survive is sometimes
mean.

cat B: a bland fellow, gets along with all the
other cats and he likes to sleep against my lower
leg at night, left leg while I'm on my back, right
leg when I'm on my belly and
he's heard Johnny Carson and maybe has seen him
but like me
he never laughs at
that.

cat C: the clown, big boy, huge eyes, he's tan and
white, the favorite of the cat hospital, they think
he's funny
but when he goes out at night
there are soon horrible screams from the
darkness.
he's killed one of the neighbors cats, mutilated
another.
he returns with tufts of fur sticking out of his

mouth, endless scratches, dried blood, swellings,
ripped tail, ripped paw, he's had one broken leg,
he's always back at the hospital, he's so often
bandaged, red and white bandages, he rips them
off, we jam antibiotic pills into his
mouth and try to keep him in at
night.
he's never read Schopenhauer but would dig hell
out of him.

cat D: the mother of cats B and C.
and all the cats chase her except B.
cat E does too but I haven't told you about cat
E.
stick around.
anyhow, cat D gets most of the love from us,
her existence is so damned, she just hides and hides
and licks her grievous wounds.
if she could read she would probably wax to the
sisters
Brontë.

cat E: just came to the door one
day, all black, the perfect animal, each movement
slides through space without friction, he's the
leopard, those yellow eyes look at you and say:
kill or be killed, he is centuries old, the other
cats stay away from him, including the great
fighter: C.
it's the EYES, they can't handle those
EYES.
he will never be tamed

yet manage to pick him up, stroke him, put him
down, he will follow you for some minutes, purring:
he is thanking you for not murdering
him.
he'd scare hell out of Charles Manson
and if he had to choose from such things
in a milder moment
he might possibly go
Celine.

anyhow, all these strange hunks of life
let us know how alone we are
forever and yet
never
so.

nevertheless, for all those cans of
tuna
A, B, C, D, and E
keep us trotting to the
supermarket

where the clerks are
all different
also.

∫

Having a bunch of cats around is good. If you're feeling bad, you just look at the cats, you'll feel better, because they know that everything is, just as it is. There's nothing to get excited about. They just know. They're saviors. The more cats you have, the longer you live. If you have a hundred cats, you'll live ten times longer than if you have ten. Someday this will be discovered, and people will have a thousand cats and live forever. It's truly ridiculous.

[. . .]

The best feeling is when you whip a guy you're not supposed to whip, I got into it with a guy one time, he was giving me a lot of lip. I said, "Okay. Let's go." He was no problem at all—I whipped him easy. He was lying there on the ground. He's got a bloody nose, the whole works. He said, "Jesus, you move slow, man. I thought you'd be easy—the goddamn fight started—I couldn't see your hands anymore, you were so fucking fast. What

happened?" I said, "I don't know, man. That's just the way it goes." You save it. You save it for the moment.

My cat, *Beeker,* is a fighter. He gets mauled up a bit sometimes, but he's always the winner. I taught him it all, you know . . . lead with the left, set up the right.

Ting, Ding, and Beeker

∫

warm light

alone
tonight
in this house,
alone with
6 cats
who tell me
without
effort
all that there
is
to know.

∫

the dream

I was having this dream I was standing in this room
and the tiniest little man
walked in.

he said
"I am the Rope Man and you are going to
strangle yourself."

I said
"oh no I'm not."

"oh yes you are,"
he told me,
"it's automatic."

in front of him was a little wooden spool
and some rope was wrapped around
it.

then in front of me was a mound of
rope

I reached down got a handful began winding it
around my neck

I tried to stop myself I
couldn't

I wound the rope tighter and tighter then began
pulling at it strangling myself.

then I heard my wife she was screaming at *Bugger*
one of our cats the young one who hadn't been fixed
yet and every morning about 5:30 a.m.
Bugger started attacking one of our other
cats.

awakened I got up and pulled *Bugger* off the other cat
carried him down the stairway opened the front door
gently eased him
outside.

then I went back upstairs got into bed decided not
to tell my wife about the dream she took such things
too seriously

but I couldn't help wondering how that dream might have
ended

Bugger might have saved my
life

for that I decided to let him keep
his balls
maybe into the
Spring.

∫

So you've got a talking cat. I mean, that's hot bananas.
And he listens to the answering machine. I've got 6
cats and not a damned one of them speaks even pid-
gin English . . . You ever thought of putting that cat
on the poetry reading circuit? Think of him doing *The
Inferno*. Or maybe he writes his own stuff. Is he fixed?
The ladies just love to blow and screw the poets. We
know that.

∫

some of this place

one hundred twenty-five thousand fools
lined up for a free hamburger in
hell and
got it.

Henry Miller jacked-off a
bull.

and in 1889
Vincent entered a
mental asylum in
St. Remy.

1564: Michelangelo, Vesalius,
Calvin die; Shakespeare, Marlowe,
Galileo
born.

caught a flounder yesterday,
cooked it
today.

in the horror of horror of
horror
works a blinding rush of

light:
tonight
when I let the
6 cats in
it was so
beautiful
that
for the smallest
moment
I
turned away
facing the east
wall.

Prana

∫

our gang

I wanted to name our cats
Ezra, Celine, Turgenev,
Ernie, Fyodor and
Gertrude
but
being a good guy
I let my wife
name them
and it came out:
Ting, Ding, Beeker,
Bhau, Feather and
Beauty.

nary a Tolstoy
in the whole bloody
batch.

∫

unclassical symphony

the cat that died
in the middle of the street

tire-crushed in non-vain
glory

it was nothing

and neither were
we

look
away.

∫

war surplus

my wife is more apprehensive than I am
and we were in this store
poking about the items when
my wife said, "I want some gas
masks."

"gas masks?"

"yes, there are all those storage tanks
by the harbor, if they bomb that there is
going to be a mass of flame and
gas."

"I never thought about that," I
said.

my wife found a clerk and sure enough he
took us to the gas masks—ugly, unwieldy
dumb-looking things.
the clerk showed us how they
operated.

"we'll take two," my wife
said.

we walked to the counter to pay.

"don't you have gas masks for cats?" my wife
asked. "we have 5 cats."

"cats?" the clerk asked.

"yes, what will the cats do if there is an
explosion?"

"lady, cats are different than we are, they
are of a lower order."

"I think cats are better than we are,"
I said.

the clerk looked at me. "we don't have
gas masks for cats."

"do you accept MasterCard?" I
asked.
"yes," he said.

the clerk took my card, ran it through, wrote
up the slip, handed it to me.

I
signed it.

"do you have any cats?" my wife asked
him.

"children," he said.

"our cats are our children," my wife
said.

the clerk bagged the masks, handed them to
me.

"don't you have any size
eleven-and-one-half sneakers?" I asked.

"no, sir."

we walked out of there.

and the clerk didn't
thank us for
our
purchase.

∫

when everything seems like suicide finality

and the Black Hearse from Hell is running through me
with its flat tires, leaky radiator, the headless
chauffeur flogging off a bag of paperclips —
stinking screams running like greyhounds through
my plastic brain bags
I
check out my 5 cats.
I check their bungholes
ears
paws
eyelashes, their
fissures, their fix, their fondle, their IBM
electricity, their
eyes bleeding from the center of the fire
and they look at me
and say through the irises: be
calm, the sea is your blood, the moon is
one of your balls — the big left one —
and your automobile sits in the garage waiting
on you patiently and
even your wife
loves you.
you are making too much of nothing, watch us
and learn the cool: brave is beautiful, we are all
together in nowhere and that's splendid, July and

circumference are the same thing
and
asshole
you don't even have to lick and scratch,
exactly.

it has worked so
far: the 5 best cats
in the world.

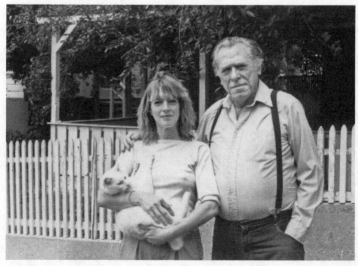

Manx

∫

I walked up the driveway. The cats were sprawled
about, pooped. In my next life I want to be a cat. To
sleep 20 hours a day and wait to be fed. To sit around
licking my ass. Humans are too miserable and angry
and single-minded.

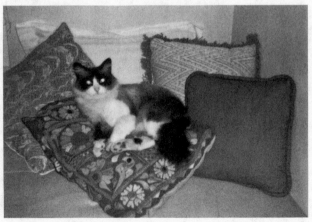

Craney

∫

cool fur

one of our fattest
cats
CRANEY
sleeps upside down
just about
anywhere
his legs sticking up
in the air.

he knows that we will
never step on
him
but doesn't know
how nervously
and incompletely we
humans
sleep.

and live.

\int

consummation

I come down the stairway and she asks,
"did you write some little
poems?"
"yes," I answer.
I sit next to her on the couch and we
both look at the t.v.
screen.
it's David Letterman.
"all the cats are in except Beeker,"
she says.
"I'll look for him," I say.
I get up and go outside and clap my
hands and yell,
"Beeker! Beeker!
come on, Beeker!"
4 or 5 people in this working-class
neighborhood curse me from under
their sheets.
Beeker comes slowly from another
yard.
he clambers the fence.
he's fat.
he drops, grunts and we walk
toward the door together,

enter.
I lock the door, turn as Letterman
vanishes into a
commercial.

Butch

∫

tragedy?

the cat sprayed on my
computer
and knocked it
out.

now I'm back to the
old
typer.

it's just
tougher.
it can handle
cat spray, spilled beer
and wine,
cigarette and
cigar ashes,
damned near
everything.

reminds me of
myself.

welcome back,
old boy,
from the
old boy.

∫

Do you have a cat? Or cats? They sleep, baby. They can sleep 20 hours a day and they look beautiful. They know that there's nothing to get excited about. The next meal. And a little something to kill now and then. When I'm being torn by the forces, I just look at one or more of my cats. There are 9 of them. I just look at one of them sleeping or half-sleeping and I relax. Writing is also my cat. Writing lets me face it. It chills me out. For a while anyhow. Then my wires get crossed and I have to do it all over again. I can't understand writers who decide to stop writing. How do they chill out?

∫

We now have 9 cats. The strays arrive and we can't turn them away. We've got to stop. Damned cats get me up early in the morning to let them out. If I don't, they start ripping up the furniture. But they are wonderful and beautiful animals. Cool. I know where the expression 'cool cat' comes from now.

∫

my cats

I know. I know.
they are limited, have different
needs and
concerns.

but I watch and learn from them.
I like the little they know,
which is so
much.

they complain but never
worry.
they walk with a surprising dignity.
they sleep with a direct simplicity that
humans just can't
understand.

their eyes are more
beautiful than our eyes.
and they can sleep 20 hours
a day
without
hesitation or
remorse.

when I am feeling
low
all I have to do is
watch my cats
and my
courage
returns.

I study these
creatures.

they are my
teachers.

Sources

A large number of the poems published in the posthumous collections, especially beginning with *What Matters Most Is How Well You Walk Through the Fire* (1999), differ—sometimes radically so—from the manuscript version of the very same poems. In an attempt to rescue Bukowski's genuine voice and style, the poems in this volume are faithful reproductions of the original manuscripts. If a given manuscript could not be found, then the appropriate magazine version was used; literary magazine editors made very few changes—if any—even printing Bukowski's unintended typographical mistakes. The sources below indicate which version is being used for each poem as well as its date of publication.

Poems flagged as uncollected have previously appeared in small press magazines only, but given their obscure nature and limited print runs—200 or 300 copies, if that—it is almost as if they were never actually published. Likewise, while some of the poems printed in this collection have appeared in previous Black Sparrow Press and Ecco volumes of poetry, the versions made available here have never been published before. This book, then, is a collection of new poetry and prose by Charles Bukowski.

∫

"All the eating places were closed . . ." Excerpt from "Aftermath of a Lengthy Rejection Slip," *Story*, March–April 1944; collected in *Portions from a Wine-Stained Notebook*, 2008.

"A cat walks by . . ." Excerpt from "poem for personnel managers," *Quixote* 13, Spring 1957.

"I don't want to draw . . ." Excerpt from "bring down the beams," *Hearse* 4, early 1959.

"conversation on a telephone." *Targets* 4, December 1960; collected in *The Days Run Away Like Wild Horses Over the Hills*, 1969.

"I saw that bird and . . ." Excerpt from a July 24, 1960, letter to Sheri Martinelli; *Beerspit Night and Cursing*, 2001.

"I saw a bird when . . ." Excerpt from a late July 1960 letter to Jory Sherman; *Screams from the Balcony*, 1993.

"the cat." c. 1960–61 manuscript; previously unpublished.

"The Arabians admire the cat . . ." Excerpt from a December 21, 1960, letter to Sheri Martinelli; *Beerspit Night and Cursing*.

"I do not always hate the cat that kills the bird, only the cat that kills me . . ." c. 1963 manuscript; previously unpublished.

"Small birds who go . . ." This line was used as a subtitle for *It Catches My Heart in Its Hands*, 1963.

"startled into life like fire." *Florida Education* 42.4, December 1964, where it was published as "startled into steam of life like fire." Collected in *Burning in Water, Drowning in Flame*, 1974.

"I was born to hustle roses down the avenues of the dead." *Crucifix in a Deathhand*, 1965.

"The factories, the jails . . ." Excerpt from an early August 1965 letter to Jim Roman; previously unpublished.

"the devious good of rescuing the suffering." *Spectroscope* 1, April 1966; previously uncollected, based on a poem titled "cat" written on November 6, 1964.

"portrait of a soul for flies." *Intermission,* September 1966; previously uncollected.

"sensible brush, sleeping . . ." Untitled poem published in *Hiram Poetry Review* 1, Fall–Winter 1966; collected as "the cat" in *The Days* . . .

"I don't like love as a command . . ." Excerpt from a November 18, 1966, letter to Carl Weissner; *Screams from the Balcony*.

"the mockingbird." April 1971 manuscript; collected in *Mockingbird Wish Me Luck*, 1972.

"looking at the cat's balls." September 7, 1971, manuscript; collected in *The People Look Like Flowers at Last*, 2007.

"the strangest thing." Early to mid-1970s manuscript; collected in *Play the Piano Drunk Like a Percussion Instrument Until the Fingers Begin to Bleed a Bit*, 1979.

"wet night." *Burning in Water, Drowning in Flame*, 1974.

"cats kill cats . . ." Excerpt from "the joke," September 15, 1975, manuscript; collected as "the cosmic joke" in *The Night Torn Mad with Footsteps*, 2001.

"little tigers everywhere." November 14, 1975, manuscript; collected in *Love Is a Dog from Hell*, 1977.

"love is the crushed cats . . ." Excerpt from "a definition," November 14, 1975, manuscript; collected in *The Night Torn* . . .

"I walked into the kitchen . . ." Excerpt from last chapter of *Women*, 1978.

"bad fix." June 13, 1978, manuscript; collected in *Dangling in Tournefortia*, 1981.

"gift." July 16, 1978, manuscript; previously uncollected.

"Butch Van Gogh." November 9, 1978, manuscript; collected in *Open All Night*, 2000.

"a reader." August 27, 1979, manuscript; previously unpublished.

"Manx." December 23, 1979, manuscript; collected in *Open All Night*.

"An international thief . . ." Excerpt from a June 10, 1981, letter to Carl Weissner; previously unpublished.

"The Manx is walking again . . ." Excerpt from a June 28, 1981, letter to Carl Weissner; previously unpublished.

"Now here's a beautiful cat . . ." Excerpt from "Charles Bukowski," an interview with Penny Grenoble; *South Bay*, November 1981; previously uncollected.

"the manx came to the door . . ." Excerpt from a January 27, 1982, letter to Louise Webb; *Screams from the Balcony*.

"night work." March 4, 1980, manuscript; collected in *Dangling* . . .

"One day I was standing around . . ." Excerpt from *Ham on Rye*, 1982.

"cats and people and you and me and everything." September 14, 1981, manuscript; collected as "in other words" in *Bone Palace Ballet*, 1997, and as "cats and you and me" in *The Night Torn* . . .

"I find my place, pull into . . ." Excerpt from a "Notes of a Dirty Old Man" column written in November 1982, posthumously published as "Death in the Afternoon" in *Betting on the Muse*, 1996.

"the history of a tough motherfucker." February 28, 1983, manuscript (second draft); collected in *War All the Time*, 1984.

"The tailless, cross-eyed cat . . ." Short note published after reprint of "the history of a tough motherfucker" in *Arete* 2.1, July/August 1989; previously uncollected.

"terminology." August 20, 1983, manuscript; collected in *War All the Time*.

"one for the old boy." August 1983 manuscript; collected in *War All the Time*.

"a nature poem for you." June 26, 1984, manuscript; collected as "an animal poem" in *The Night Torn* . . .

"a sensible fellow." October 1984 manuscript; previously uncollected.

"wearing the collar." March 1985 manuscript; collected in *You Get So Alone at Times That It Just Makes Sense*, 1986.

"exactly fine." November 15, 1985, manuscript; collected as "exactly right" in *The Night Torn* . . .

"In the morning we awakened . . ." Excerpt from *The Wedding*, November 1985 manuscript; previously uncollected.

"a cat is a cat is a cat is a cat." *Wormwood Review* 128, 1992; previously published in *You Get So Alone* . . .

"another casualty." *You Get So Alone* . . .

"my cat, the writer." June 18, 1986, manuscript; collected in *The Night Torn* . . .

"5 cats." c. 1986 manuscript; previously unpublished.

"Having a bunch of cats . . ." Excerpt from "Tough Guys Write Poetry," an interview with Sean Penn; *Interview,* September 1987.

"warm light." *Warm Light* bookmark, September 1990; collected in *The Last Night of the Earth Poems*, 1992.

"the dream." January 16, 1990, manuscript; previously uncollected.

"So you've got a talking cat . . ." Excerpt from a January 28, 1990, letter to William Packard; *Reach for the Sun*, 1999.

"some of this place." May 7, 1990, manuscript; collected as "this place" in *Sifting Through the Madness for the Word, the Line, the Way*, 2003.

"our gang." November 25, 1990, manuscript; previously uncollected.

"unclassical symphony." December 31, 1990, manuscript; collected in *Sifting Through the Madness* . . .

"war surplus." c. 1990 manuscript; collected as "military surplus" in *Slouching Toward Nirvana*, 2005.

"when everything seems like suicide finality." *Raccoon* 30/31, September 1991; previously uncollected.

"I walked up the driveway . . ." Excerpt from an October 2, 1991, journal entry published in *The Captain Is Out to Lunch and the Sailors Have Taken Over the Ship*, 1998.

"cool fur." October 23, 1991, manuscript; collected in *Bone Palace Ballet*, 1997.

"consummation." c. early 1990s manuscript; collected in *The Continual Condition*, 2009.

"tragedy?" *New York Quarterly* 49, 1992; collected as "reunion" in *Bone Palace Ballet*, and in *The Continual Condition*.

"Do you have a cat? . . ." Excerpt from an April 16, 1992, journal entry published in *The Captain Is Out* . . .

"We now have 9 cats . . ." Excerpt from an October 13, 1992, letter to Louise Webb; *Reach for the Sun.*

"my cats." c. 1989 manuscript; collected in *Come on In*, 2006.

Acknowledgments

The editor and publisher would like to thank the owners of the material here printed, which include the following institutions:
 University of Arizona, Special Collections Center
 The University of California, Santa Barbara, Special Collections
 The Huntington Library, San Marino, California
 The State University of New York at Buffalo, Poetry/Rare
 Book Collection
 Temple University, Special Collections

Thanks also to the following magazines, where some of the poems and stories were first printed: *Arete, Florida Education, Hiram Poetry Review, Intermission, Raccoon, Spectroscope, Story, Targets,* and *Wormwood Review.*

Mistery